coffee

discovering, exploring, enjoying

coffee

discovering, exploring, enjoying

hattie ellis

photography by debi treloar

RYLAND
PETERS
& SMALL
LONDON NEW YORK

*To Clare Moberly, who at the time of writing
drinks the brew in Brazil.*

Designer Luis Peral-Aranda
Senior Editor Sophie Bevan
Picture Research Manager Kate Brunt
Production Tamsin Curwood
Art Director Gabriella Le Grazie
Publishing Director Alison Starling

Stylist Emily Chalmers
Food Stylist Fiona Smith

First published in Great Britain in 2002
by Ryland Peters & Small
Kirkman House
12–14 Whitfield Street
London W1T 2RP
www.rylandpeters.com

10 9 8 7 6 5 4 3 2

ISBN 1 84172 348 7

Printed and bound in China

contents

what is coffee?

Coffee beans are the seeds inside the cherries of an evergreen plant that grows in the humid lands between the tropic of Cancer and the tropic of Capricorn. After the cherries are harvested and processed to remove the outer layers, the green beans travel around the world. Roasted, ground and mixed with hot water, their concentrated, aromatic flavours are released to make one of the most remarkable and celebrated drinks in the world. Utterly transformed from plant to cup, the tastes – of lemon, of blueberries, of wine – that lie within this bitter black brew can still remind you of its origins at the heart of a fruit.

Ancient as tribes and irrepressibly modern, coffee adapts itself to time and place, encompassing the romantic, the industrious and the day-to-day. Its dynamic history is full of tales of passion and intrigue, yet it is also the drink of breakfast and of mid-morning office breaks. Prized for its intriguing range of flavours and styles, used as a digestive, relied upon as a stimulant, coffee excites and focuses the brain along with the rest of the body. It brings us together over cups and conversation. Its aromatic allure can beckon us away from our daily business to a café for a quiet sip, a newspaper and a view of the world. Solitary or sociable, it allows us both to unwind and to recharge.

The current surge of interest in coffee has developed through a growing awareness of the quality end of the market, in freshly roasted beans that have a particular provenance and a distinctive taste, and in the many ways of drinking coffee, such as cappuccino and espresso. This book celebrates coffee in all its forms and looks at how to discover and enjoy its many flavours and possibilities.

The outer layers of the cherries from the coffee plant are removed (above and opposite, below right) to get the green beans. These can be transported around the world and are then roasted, ground and added to hot water to make coffee.

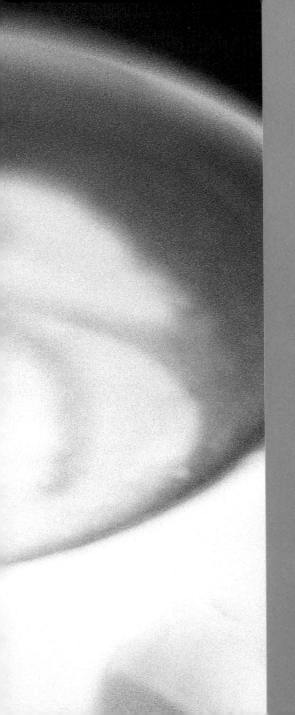

Coffee drinking began in Ethiopia and spread to Arabia and the Islamic world before travelling around the rest of the globe. The black brew stirred up a storm of interest wherever it went, as people took to this new drink with its remarkable ability to awake and refresh both mind and body.

the buzz

the origins of coffee

Ethiopia, believed by many to be the ancient birthplace of mankind, is where coffee's long history begins. Legend tells of a goatherd in Abyssinia called Kaldi who noticed his animals prancing around after nibbling at the leaves and fruit of particular bushes. So it was that, right from the start, the plant was recognized and prized as a stimulant. Monks took coffee to keep them awake for nocturnal prayers, and travellers rolled the cherries with fat into balls to make an early trail food.

Coffea arabica was cultivated by the Arabs, who used coffee as both a medicine and as a pleasurable stimulant. Coffee houses sprang up where people would meet to drink, play backgammon, talk and listen to music and storytelling. Pilgrims and traders spread the bean around the Muslim world, and its fame – and consumption – spanned North Africa, Turkey and Persia.

Although coffee was initially prized by the religious, the coffee houses came to be regarded as subversive – as places of temptation and ideological ferment – and the early history of coffee is full of stories of suppression. Yet its progress around the world was indefatigable, as people discovered this *qahwa al-bon*, 'wine of the bean', that could waken mind, spirit and senses.

spread around the world

Coffee consumption really took off in the West from the 17th century onwards. One of the bean's earliest European destinations was the trade centre of Venice, which received coffee with other goods from the East. At first, Italian Christian leaders rejected the drink as darkly satanic and wanted it excommunicated. But Pope Clement VIII took a sip, realised this delectable taste was here to stay, and blessed the new brew as heavenly instead.

Bags of green beans were left behind by the Turks, who had besieged Vienna in 1683. Franz George Kolschitzky, a Pole who went behind enemy lines for the Austrians, became a double hero when he showed how the beans could be turned into a drink – Viennese coffee and the Viennese café were born.

Coffee houses popularized the drink wherever it was consumed. Coinciding with the start of newspapers and the thinking of the Enlightenment, coffee became known as 'the drink of democracy'. British coffee houses were referred to as 'penny universities' because, for the price of a cup of coffee, people could meet, talk and participate in the political and philosophical discussions of the day. 'The history of coffee houses,' wrote Isaac D'Israeli, '… was that of the manners, the morals and the politics of a people.' These meeting places often attracted specific groups of people; and institutions still in existence today, such as the insurers Lloyds of London, began as coffee houses.

The first French café, Café Procope, opened its doors opposite the Comédie Française in 1689, and soon became the haunt of philosophers, writers and political activists. By the end of the 18th century there were 800 cafés in Paris and by 1843 there were 3,000.

After the Boston Tea Party, Americans saw tea as 'unpatriotic' and became a nation of coffee drinkers. The bean, now grown outside Africa and Arabia, arrived in Latin America, which was to become the biggest producer of coffee in the world, on the doorstep of the booming US market.

NI, BOURBON:

COLOMBIA

AGUNA:
RICA

DJIMMAH:
A

1·3Kg – 3Kg	3Kg – 5·5Kg
12·50 Per KILO	11·20 Per KILO

THE KIRIMARA ESTATE KENYA

Up to 450g	450g – 1·3Kg	1·3Kg – 3Kg	3Kg – 5·5Kg
20 Per Kg	17·40 Per Kg	15·90 Per Kg	14·50 Per Kg

...TUSION = NICARAGUA

...COTEGTIVO = PERU

THE ASARO ESTATE = PAPUA NEW GUINEA

...JIMAH ESTATE = JAVA

Up to 450g	450g – 1·3Kg	1·3Kg – 3Kg	3Kg – 5·5Kg
16·60 Per KILO	14·00 Per KILO	13·00 Per KILO	11·65 Per KILO

SAN AGUSTIN : COLOMBIA

MOUNT RAMALU : TIMOR EAST

MEDELLIN EXCELSO WATER PROCESS : DECAFFEINATED COLO

[O...] ESPRESSO BLEND

Up to 450g	450g – 1·3Kg	1·3Kg – 3Kg	3Kg –
18·80 Per KILO	15·90 Per KILO	14·65 Per KILO	13·20

ESPRESSO BLEND

Up to 450g	450g – 1·3Kg	1·3Kg – 3Kg	3Kg –
17·70 Per Kg	15·00 Per Kg	13·80 Per Kg	12·

SPECIAL

coffee trade

Coffee grows on vast Brazilian plantations and is collected from the wild in Ethiopian forests; it is cultivated on the ancient terraces carved into the steep mountainsides of Yemen and on Indonesian smallholdings, where the beans can still be spread out to dry on the roadside. All these beans, and many others besides, make their way into markets, local and global. In volume, coffee is the second most traded commodity in the world, after oil.

Coffee production can be affected by political upheaval, when growers may switch from export crops to subsistence farming, and it is prone to the natural disasters such as frost, earthquakes, hurricanes and floods that can devastate the Tropics. The price fluctuations that affect any global commodity can mean disaster to the small grower, which is why the Fairtrade movement (see page 62) guarantees a stable price that goes directly to the producer and enables them to continue farming in a sustainable way.

Some of the best coffees from around the world end up on the high street in specialist coffee merchants. These professionals, and the wholesalers who supply them, have the skill, experience and contacts to source consistently good beans from the market, tasting each new crop and roasting every batch of beans to perfection to bring out their optimum flavours. They will create and maintain house blends, supply you with your favourite coffees and enable you to explore a wider range of beans. Follow the tantalizing aroma that wisps out through the door of a good coffee shop or café, and it will lead you to a whole world of flavour.

famous coffee drinkers

Coffee gives people energy, and cafés bring them together – a potent combination that has long whirred the wheels of political, creative and philosophical revolutions. Voltaire downed as many as 50 cups a day. Beethoven would count 60 beans into a single cup. The writing of Goethe's *Sorrows of Young Werther* was fuelled by caffeine. Balzac would walk across Paris to get three kinds of coffee from different shops to make his favoured blend that kept him awake to write from midnight until midday. He explained that when he drank coffee, '… ideas begin to move. Things remembered arrive at full gallop … the shafts of wit start up like sharp-shooters. Similes arise, the paper is covered in ink ….'

The Boston Tea Party was planned in secrecy at the Green Dragon coffee house. And, just a few years later, in 1789, Desmoulins whipped up a revolutionary crowd when he leapt onto a table to speak from the Café Foy in Paris; two days later, the Bastille was stormed.

'Strong coffee, and plenty, awakens me,' said Napoleon, who favoured a Brazilian Santos-Mocha blend. 'It gives me warmth, an unusual force, a pain that is not without pleasure. I would rather suffer than be senseless.'

Jean Paul Sartre and Simone de Beauvoir wrote at Les Deux Magots, a quintessential Left Bank café, whilst the Beat Poets drank coffee and talked the talk at the Caffe Trieste and the Co-Existence Bagel Shop in San Fransisco. Impressionism, Surrealism, Cubism, Existentialism – all these movements brewed in the atmosphere of cafés and coffee shops. Alcohol may incite the passions, but coffee engenders both excitement and action.

roasts and blends

Coffee is exported as green beans. These are sent around the world in sacks, and are then roasted by specialists to bring out their subtle flavours. As the beans heat up and turn a glossy brown, the oils develop that are the secret of their marvellous flavour.

Roasts vary from light brown through medium to the very dark beans favoured by the French and Italians. Light roasts, such as 'cinnamon', have a more delicate, mildly aromatic taste. Medium roasts, also known as 'city' or 'American', are slightly stronger. Viennese roasts are a little darker than medium, while French, Italian and Continental roasts edge into deep brown and near-black, producing enticingly bitter, richly pungent flavours, such as those found in espresso.

The art of blending is to marry different beans together to create a harmonious balance of flavours, acidity and body. Specialist coffee merchants pride themselves on their variations on classics, such as mellow breakfast blends, stronger after-dinner blends and those used to make espresso. One long-standing combination is Mocha-Java, which combines aroma and strength to make a delicious, potent brew. It takes skill and constant tasting to create and maintain house blends, as even beans from the same place will vary from batch to batch and from year to year.

Since the plant was first cultivated commercially on the continent in the 18th century, the Americas have become the largest producers of coffee in the world. Costa Rican beans are highly prized for their fragrant flavours, balance and entrancing acidity. Tarrazu is the most famous region, producing excellent coffee, in a land known as the 'Switzerland of coffee countries' for its consistency, clean flavours and attention to detail. This is a good place to source high-altitude beans, such as the high-grade Strictly Hard Bean (SHB).

For a contrast in style, the rugged terrain and remote highlands of Guatemala produce smoky, chocolatey, fruity beans loved for their distinctive individuality. Look out for beans such as those from isolated Huehuetenango, the volcanic slopes above the city of Antigua and the moist climate of Cobán.

Brazil grows around a third of the world's coffee, much of it on vast plantations stretching in broad sweeps to the horizon. Specialists hunt out high-grade Brazilian coffees, such as those from the older Bourbon plant. Colombia, the second largest coffee producer in the world, is known for the full-bodied, mellow consistency of its washed coffees, from the *supremo* (large) and *excelso* (smaller) beans.

Mexico produces nutty beans with Central American acidity, and is known for its elephantine Maragogype beans. Nicaragua and El Salvador, recovering from political upheaval, are now exporting interesting coffees. Hawaii has the smooth, complex Kona coffees; and Jamaican Blue Mountain is famous for its high-quality beans which command equally high prices.

Africa

Some coffee grows wild in its indigenous landscape of Ethiopia, and the beans produced from this ancient land intrigue drinkers with their winey, gamey, perfumed flavours and aromatic hints of apricots, blueberries, lemon, grapes and flowers. Look out for coffees such as those from Harrar and from the Sidamo region, which may be labelled after the town of Yirgacheffe. Likely to be grown without pesticides or artificial fertilizers, the natural wildness of these coffee plants translates into the cup as rare, interesting coffees.

Across the Red Sea, Yemeni coffees share some of the same characteristics and may be called Mocha, after the port in Yemen which exported early coffees to Europe. These beans of Arabia can be perfumed with a heavy-bodied piquancy and a bright acidity. Dry-processed, they can be earthy with an almost liquorice tang. Mattari and Sanani coffees are the best known.

Grown high up, some at over 1,500 metres (5,000 feet), Kenyan coffees can stop you in your tracks with their pure, fresh, tangy tastes. Kenyan beans are loved for their balance of beautiful body, clean acidity and berry fruitiness. The top-grade beans are graded AA, and are wet-processed. Kenyan Peaberries, with their single fruit, are a speciality and have a satisfyingly rounded appearance and a smooth, sometimes malty, taste.

Other African countries known for their coffees include Tanzania, Zimbabwe and Malawi, which can all have the sparkling acidity and fruity flavours of the East African coffee style.

Asia

The Dutch first grew coffee on the Indonesian island of Java, and its name has been used to refer to all the coffees from this country, and, historically, for coffee in general. Javanese coffees are known for their earthy, spicy, rich flavours. Sumatra and Sulawesi also grow luscious, full-bodied coffees with strong, distinctive flavours of herbs, woods, spices and even syrupy-smooth caramel. Sulawesi coffees are sometimes sold under the former Dutch name for the island, Celebes.

One intriguing, and expensive, Indonesian speciality is the Kopi Luak coffee, made from beans eaten and excreted by a small, cat-like wild animal, the luak. The beans, transformed in the animal's digestive tract, have,

as you might imagine, something of a cult following. Some Indonesian coffees are aged to mimic the taste acquired when the beans were stockpiled in this damp, warm climate or underwent long sea voyages to the West. Neighbouring Papua New Guinea produces coffees with a perfumed tropical fruitiness.

Coffee has been grown in India since as early as the 17th century and specialities include aged Monsoon coffees, where the beans are exposed to the monsoon winds in open warehouses; the result is a coffee with a special, mellow flavour. Southern India grows other coffees with enticing scents of spices. Mysore coffees are one kind known for quality, as they come from a state where arabica plants are grown.

flavoured and decaf

Certain flavours such as vanilla and chocolate have an affinity with coffee, hence the chocolate on the top of a cappuccino, or the delicious addition of a spoonful of vanilla sugar to an after-dinner cup. Spiced coffees are a traditional brew in the Middle East, where the grounds may be mixed with cardamom and other flavours, like cinnamon, nutmeg and cloves. On parts of the Amalfi coast in Italy, they sometimes add a twist of peel from their famous lemons, and the habit has followed some of the Italians living in America. Modern flavoured coffees use essential oils and other flavourings to make such brews as tiramisu, pecan nut and raspberries and cream. You can also buy or make flavoured sugar syrups to add to brewed coffees (orange is a good one), or add a dash of a liqueur for an extra tasty kick.

Decaffeinated coffees are made by dissolving the caffeine out of the bean using chemical solvents or water. Look for decaf sold by people who care about quality. Some of the taste disappears with the caffeine so you need coffee made from beans with plenty of flavour in the first place. Lesser merchants use cheap, less-delicious beans to compensate for the cost of the decaffeination process, and this is one reason why the drink can taste underpowered in more than one sense. Robusta coffees, incidentally, have about twice as much caffeine in them as the higher-quality arabicas.

Whether you like the short, black blast of espresso, the clean smoothness of filter coffee or milky sips of cappuccino, this section guides you through the practicalities of making coffee, from shopping to sipping, and looks at how its flavours can be used in food.

the brew

buying and storing

Coffee becomes infinitely more appealing and interesting if you buy from a specialist coffee shop. You can purchase through the internet and by mail order, or steep yourself in the sensory delight of the shop itself with all the entrancing aromas and busy sounds: the grinding, the chinking, the shake, rattle and roll of the beans. A good retailer will have an interesting choice of high-quality beans; they may well do their own roasting, or get a good roaster to do it to their specification, and will be able to give you advice on what to try, so expanding your enjoyment to a wider range of tastes.

Freshness is the key to good coffee. The aromatic oils start to disappear immediately after roasting so it is best to buy smaller amounts of freshly roasted coffee regularly, instead of a large amount in one go. Buy your coffee as you would other fresh foods, and use it at its peak. When beans are freshly roasted, the grounds tend to foam up when you add water.

Ideally, buy whole beans and grind them at home, as the oils lose their volatile aromas even more quickly once the coffee is ground. A proper retailer will grind the beans for you, but, best of all, do it yourself, just before brewing. An inexpensive propeller-blade grinder is a good way to start, or pay more for a burr grinder which mills the coffee between discs to get a more even grind, and has settings that can be adjusted for different grades, from coarse to fine.

Coffee should be stored in an airtight, dry container, in a cool cupboard rather than in the fridge. You can also freeze beans in an air-free bag for a couple of months, and grind them whilst still frozen.

secrets to the perfect cup

Making coffee correctly allows you to really taste the full, fresh and interesting flavours on offer. These four straightforward principles make all the difference between insipid meekness or brutish bitterness, and aromatic energy.

• Buy freshly roasted, good-quality whole beans and grind them just before brewing.

• The grind should be right for whatever method you are using (espresso, plunge-pot, filter or otherwise – see pages 38–41).

• Measure the amount of coffee and water used and the length of time the coffee brews. Getting the proper proportion of coffee to water and letting them brew together for the right amount of time means you extract the most character and aromatic oils from the beans without the brew becoming bitter. If you want weaker coffee, it is better to add hot water to properly brewed coffee than to use too much water or too few beans.

• With the exception of Middle Eastern coffee (which is boiled), pour the water onto the grounds when it is just off the boil. This dissolves the soluble flavours from the coffee without scalding the subtleties into bitterness. Do not keep coffee warm on the heat or it will become bitter and stewed.

The following pages outline the various methods of making the perfect cup, so you can be sure to get the right pressure in your espresso machine and the perfect froth on your cappuccino.

espresso know-how

Espresso works on the principle of forcing hot water through finely ground, dark-roasted coffee under pressure so that it blasts through the grounds, extracting the maximum flavour. The water emulsifies with the oils from the beans to make a drink that is lusciously full-bodied and rich in flavour.

At home, Italians tend to make stove-top espressos. The Moka stove-top is the classic model and there are now many others available. These pots are designed to brew a particular amount of coffee and range in size from those for a couple of cups to larger pots for more people. Fill the bottom half with water up to the rivet on the side and fill the coffee container up to the brim with finely ground coffee, levelling it off gently without compressing it, or the water will not be able to get through evenly. Screw the top part onto the bottom as tightly as possible to prevent leakage. When the coffee is ready, you will hear the bubbling, breathy 'ploff-ploff-ploff' of air being forced through the connecting tube, once all the water has gone through.

If you want to buy a domestic espresso machine, try to find one that provides high pressure, such as the pump-action models, as they get more flavour from the coffee. The more expensive machines get closer to the sophisticated engineering of the professional models in cafés. You can buy machines with convenient little ready-to-use pods of ground coffee, but this restricts your choice and the beans will not be freshly ground.

filters, cafetières and more ...

All these methods require 2 tablespoons of coffee per 180 ml water and need to brew for around four to six minutes to extract the fullest flavour from the beans.

• The most primitive method is to put coarsely ground coffee in a jug, pour over the hot water, give the mixture a stir and leave to infuse for about five or six minutes. You can wrap the jug in a tea towel and put a saucer on top to retain the heat and aromas.

- The popular plunge-pot, or cafetière, produces coffee full of the luscious aromatic oils of the coffee bean. Use coarsely ground coffee and give the coffee a stir once you have poured on the water. Infuse for four minutes. Again, you can wrap a tea towel around the pot to keep the liquid hot whilst brewing, or use an insulated plunge-pot.

- When making filter coffee, wet the medium-fine ground coffee first with a little hot water to help the water filter through evenly. If making filter coffee by hand rather than in a machine, add the water slowly to allow it to extract the flavour from the beans. This should take about four minutes. Give the coffee a stir before serving, so the flavours of the brew are equally dispersed.

- Old-fashioned French drip pots work on the same principle as filter coffee and come in three parts: a pot, a filter with holes, and a top section with a lid. You put medium-ground coffee in the filter, pour water into the top part and let it drip through to the bottom.

- Recently revived, the vacuum-pot method requires a medium-fine grind and produces coffee with a beautiful clarity of flavour.

milk and sugar?

Milk goes with coffee in many different and delicious ways. The main principle is that hot milk works better than cold. For this reason, French waiters simultaneously pour a black jet of coffee from one pot and hot milk from another to form a *café au lait*, and an Italian 'stains' an espresso with a drop of steamed milk to make a *caffè macchiato* or adds it, half and half, to make a latte.

Milk softens and alters flavours. When trying a new kind of bean, taste the drink first without milk to get a better grasp of its subtleties, then add the milk and taste once more to judge how its character is altered.

Steamed, frothy milk floats on the top of the cup giving a combination of black silk and white velvet in each sip. Double or single cream are other ways to add a seductive layer of smoothness to your cup.

Sugar takes away some of the bitterness in coffee, though well-made coffee has a subtle, glancing, alert edge of bitterness and does not call for sweetness in the same way as a brutish, stewed brew. Some like to add a spoonful to dark-roasted coffee, such as espresso, but not to lighter styles. Eating little sticky cakes or sugared biscuits with your coffee is, of course, another excellent way to sweeten the moment.

cappuccino, latte and au lait ...

The classic cappuccino is made using one third espresso, one third steamed milk and one third foam. Espresso machines usually have a metal wand which steams and froths the milk. You can also buy little electric gadgets which quickly whisk up hot milk so it doubles or trebles in volume. Alternatively, heat up milk in a saucepan or microwave and then whisk by hand until it froths. You can buy special milk-frothing whisks. Some of these come with containers you can put in the microwave to heat up the milk. Pour the hot milk onto the coffee, holding back the froth with a spoon, and add the frothed milk last. If desired, top off the cappuccino with powdered chocolate.

You can also drink a *cappuccino senza schiuma* (without foam) or a *cappuccino chiaro*, with less coffee and more milk, or the darker *cappuccino scuro*, with less milk. Just use your eye and your tastebuds to judge the proportions.

A caffè latte is made from roughly half hot or steamed milk and half espresso mixed together. The French *café au lait* is the same, except made with filter coffee.

coffee drinking and café society

From the breakfast wake-up jolt to the after-dinner digestive, coffee is consumed all around the world, morning, noon and night. There are many reasons for coffee's widespread popularity, from the medical to the gastronomic. But whether drunk by Bedouin tribesmen around a fire or by city office workers grabbing a cardboard cup between meetings, at base coffee's appeal comes from being a source of energy. Weight for weight, there is less caffeine in coffee than in tea; but cup for cup, coffee wins the race. Caffeine is quickly absorbed into your bloodstream and provides a stretch of mental alertness and focus that makes you feel as efficiently active and ready to rev as a well-oiled engine.

Each country has evolved different places where people can drink, meet and take a break, from the zinc-topped counters of French cafés and the wood-panelled, well-worn sophistication of the Viennese coffee house, to the fast, bright zap of the modern coffee chain. Café society is about people meeting, thinking, writing, talking and watching – or simply sitting in amiable surroundings with the company of a cup of coffee and a slice of cake, taking time out, in sips.

coffee and cream cheesecake

This cheesecake, with its glossy white top, shows off the classic combination of coffee and cream.

175 g digestives or wholewheat biscuits, about 11

75g butter

1 tablespoon caster sugar

Coffee filling

2 tablespoons ground coffee

500 g cream cheese

4 egg yolks

200 g caster sugar

150 ml double cream

1 vanilla pod

2 egg whites

Topping

350 ml sour cream

a springform cake tin, 20 cm diameter, lightly greased with butter

a baking sheet

serves 8–10

To make the base, put the digestives into a plastic bag and crush them finely with a rolling pin. Melt the butter in a saucepan, then stir in the crushed digestives and sugar. Press the mixture into the base of the prepared cake tin, then press it evenly about 4 cm up the sides. Bake in a preheated oven at 200°C (400°F) Gas 6 for 10 minutes, then remove from the oven and let cool. Reduce the oven temperature to 160°C (325°F) Gas 3.

Meanwhile, to make the filling, put the ground coffee into a cup, add 150 ml boiling water and let cool.

Put the cream cheese into a bowl and stir so it loosens slightly. Stir in the egg yolks, one at a time, then the sugar, then the double cream. Slit the vanilla pod down one side and, using a teaspoon or knife, scrape out the seeds into the cream cheese mixture and stir well. Stir 100 ml of the cooled coffee into the mixture.

Put the egg whites into a clean, greasefree bowl and whisk until soft peaks form. Fold into the cream cheese mixture, then spoon into the prepared cake tin set on the baking sheet. Bake at 160°C (325°F) Gas 3 for 1 hour. Leave, with the oven turned off and the door closed, for another 30 minutes. Remove from the oven and transfer to a wire rack. Reheat the oven to 220°C (425°F) Gas 7.

To make the topping, put the sour cream into a bowl and stir to loosen. Spoon over the cheesecake, spreading it out with a palette knife to get a smooth, even layer. Cook in the reheated oven for 6–7 minutes, to set the sour cream (it will form a white, glossy topping that contrasts nicely with the pale, coffee-coloured cheesecake).

Remove from the oven and let cool. Run a knife around the outside of the cheesecake, then unclip the tin (it is important to run the knife around the cheesecake, or you risk splitting it when you release the spring). Serve with coffee.

Italian coffee drinking

Hot shots of coffee fuel the animated Italians. It seems to suit their speed and spirit: even the buzzing Vespas seem to run on espresso. All through the day, you see people stopping off to stand at a bar for *un caffè* (an espresso) to recharge their batteries and go, go, go again.

The cappuccino is a milky breakfast brew that may be drunk with a *cornetto* (a croissant) or another pastry. The drink – with its hood of steamed, frothed milk – is named after the colour of the habit of the Capuchin monks, who, in turn, were named after the hoods (*cappuccio*) of their habits.

The classic espresso is a very short measure – just a few long, deliciously bitter sips – and a well-made one has a pale brown foam, or *crema*, on top. A double espresso (*caffè doppio*) is a double measure. A *caffè lungo* has more water for a less strong drink and a *caffè ristretto* has less water for a stronger brew. A *caffè macchiato* has a dollop of steamed milk, whilst a *latte macchiato* is milk with a drop of coffee.

On hot days, you can refresh yourself with a *caffè freddo* or iced coffee, or make that a *caffè latte freddo* with the addition of milk. And on a cold day, or after a meal, you could add a drop of spirits for a fortifying, warming *caffè corretto*.

Don't toast all the almonds – reserve a few untoasted to use as a pale decoration on the brown ice cream. Alternatively, cut some of the toasted almonds into thin shards to sprinkle over each serving.

coffee and almond ice cream

300 ml double cream

300 ml full-cream milk

3 tablespoons coarsely ground coffee (grind for 8–12 seconds)

100 g flaked almonds, plus 2 tablespoons for decoration (optional)

4 large egg yolks

100 g sugar

a baking sheet

an ice-cream maker or freezer trays

serves 4–6

Put the cream and milk into a heavy-based saucepan. Add the coffee and stir over a low heat for 5 minutes, without boiling, to infuse the flavours. Remove from the heat and let cool for 10 minutes, then strain the mixture through a sieve lined with damp muslin into a bowl.

Put the almonds onto the baking sheet and toast them in a preheated oven at 200°C (400°F) Gas 6, checking after a couple of minutes and giving them a shake. The nuts are ready when pale brown and smelling sweet and toasty.

Put the egg yolks and sugar into a heatproof bowl and whisk well. Reheat the coffee cream, without boiling, then whisk it into the beaten eggs, a little at a time.

Put the bowl over a saucepan of simmering water and stir constantly with a wooden spoon until the mixture thickens slightly (it will thicken more as it cools). You can also do this in a heavy-based saucepan directly over very low heat. (If the mixture curdles, strain it to remove the strands of solidified egg.) Stir in the toasted almonds.

Remove from the heat and cool the mixture by putting the bowl into a larger bowl of cold water. When cool, chill in the refrigerator until quite cold. Churn in an ice cream maker, according to the manufacturer's instructions. Alternatively, part-freeze the mixture in shallow trays, then remove and beat to break down the ice crystals. Part-freeze and beat again – the more you do this, the smoother the ice cream will be. Freeze until solid.

Serve plain, or topped with the reserved almonds, if using.

mocha truffle tart

Serve this intensely flavoured tart slightly warm from the oven.

100 g plain flour

1 tablespoon cocoa powder

2 tablespoons caster sugar

50 g unsalted butter, cut into small cubes

1 large egg yolk, beaten

crème fraîche or sour cream, to serve

coffee and chocolate filling

250 g plain chocolate (at least 70 per cent cocoa solids), chopped

3 teaspoons instant espresso powder

3 large egg yolks

1 large whole egg

50 g caster sugar

a loose-bottom tart tin, 22 cm diameter

foil and baking beans or rice

serves 6

To make the pastry, sift the flour, cocoa and sugar into a bowl. Add the cubes of butter and, using your fingertips, rub them into the dry ingredients until the mixture looks like breadcrumbs. Add 1 tablespoon water and the beaten egg yolk. Stir the mixture with a knife, then, using your fingertips, gently draw it together into a ball. Chill for at least 1 hour.

Transfer the chilled pastry to a floured work surface and roll out as thinly as possible. Drape the pastry over the rolling pin, then drape it over the prepared tart tin. Press it into the corners of the tin, then trim the edges of the pastry and flute it with your fingers. Chill for at least 30 minutes.

Remove from the refrigerator and line with foil, then fill with baking beans or rice. Bake in a preheated oven at 180°C (350°F) Gas 4 for 20 minutes, then remove the beans and foil and return the pastry case to the oven for another 5 minutes to dry out the base. This is called 'baking blind'. Remove from the oven and keep the oven at the same temperature.

Meanwhile, to make the filling, put the chocolate into a heatproof bowl set over a saucepan of gently simmering water (do not let any water or steam touch the chocolate or it will be spoiled). Stir in the espresso powder.

Put the egg yolks, whole egg and caster sugar into a bowl and, using an electric hand mixer or wire whisk, whisk until light, fluffy and doubled in volume. Stir in the chocolate and coffee mixture, then pour into the pastry case. This mixture sets like lava, with every bump and ridge in evidence, so if you want an even appearance, use a knife dipped in hot water to smooth over the top.

Bake for 15 minutes (no longer, or it will dry out). Serve warm, with a dollop of crème fraîche or sour cream.

These 'kisses' are delicate walnut and coffee biscuits joined with a rich chocolate-coffee ganache.

walnut coffee kisses

40 g walnut halves or pieces
100 g unsalted butter
70 g caster sugar
½ beaten egg
110 g self-raising flour
1 teaspoon instant espresso powder

Ganache

100 g chocolate
40 g unsalted butter
125 ml double cream
1½ teaspoons instant espresso powder

2 baking sheets covered with non-stick baking parchment

makes 24 biscuits, 12 'kisses'

Pre-heat oven to 180°C (350°F) Gas 4. Finely chop the walnuts – this is best done with a knife to stop the nuts becoming oily.

Put the butter and sugar into a bowl and beat until creamy. Stir in the beaten egg and then fold in the sifted flour. Stir in the espresso power, then the chopped walnuts. Put an even number (about 24) tablespoons of the mixture onto baking trays covered with non-stick parchment. Bake for about 10 minutes, or until light-brown around the edges. Remove from the oven and let cool and firm up on the tray for a couple of minutes, then carefully transfer to a wire rack to cool completely.

Meanwhile, to make the ganache, break the chocolate into pieces and put into a saucepan. Heat with butter and cream without boiling, until the butter melts. Beat in the espresso powder. Remove from the heat and stir. The mixture will thicken as it cools. Carefully sandwich the cool, fragile biscuits together with the ganache.

Middle Eastern coffee

An *ibrik*, or *kanaka*, is the tapered pot with a long handle and a pouring lip used in the Middle Eastern method of boiling coffee with water. Mix one or two heaped teaspoons of very, very finely ground coffee with an equal amount of sugar for each demitasse (little cup) of water. The *ibrik* must be only half full as the mixture will expand as it boils. Bring to the boil over a medium heat, then reduce the heat to low. Bring to the boil again, then either turn the heat off, or repeat the boiling once more.

Half-fill the cups with coffee, then add some of the prized foam to the top of each drink. For an extra-aromatic brew, use Middle Eastern coffee that is ready-mixed with cardamom.

spiced orange coffee syrup

A syrup for ice cream spiced with the cardamom that often flavours Middle Eastern coffee.

10 green cardamom pods
250 g sugar
125 ml strong coffee or espresso
1 teaspoon finely grated orange zest
1 cinnamon stick, broken into pieces

serves 6–8

Crush the cardamom pods with a knife and scrape out the seeds. Put the sugar into a heavy-bottomed saucepan, add 60 ml water and heat very slowly until the sugar dissolves – gently draw a spoon across the sugar to help the process. When all the sugar has dissolved, boil for 2 minutes, then stir in the coffee, orange zest, cinnamon and cardamom. Let cool so the flavours infuse, then strain and store the syrup in an airtight jar in the refrigerator.

To serve, pour over vanilla or chocolate ice cream.

coffee and alcohol

Coffee is often served at the end of a meal and it combines beautifully with spirits, either drunk alongside one another, or in the same cup. To make the classic Irish coffee, pour Irish whiskey (other spirits work well, too) into a glass with a spoonful of sugar, add strong, hot coffee and pour on double cream over a spoon so it floats on top. Alternatively, simply add a drop of brandy, Calvados, grappa or any number of liqueurs for an extra glow of heat to black or white coffee. Rum and orange-flavoured liqueurs such as Cointreau work particularly well.

iced coffee

You can add a splash of a liqueur such as Cointreau or rum to this deliciously refreshing drink.

2 tablespoons ground coffee

4 ice cubes

1 small scoop vanilla or chocolate ice cream (optional)

125 ml milk

1 teaspoon sugar, or to taste

a dash of liqueur (optional)

serves 1

Make the coffee using your normal method, but make it stronger than usual (2 tablespoons ground coffee to 125 ml water) because it will be diluted by the ice cubes. When brewed, pour the coffee over the ice cubes. As an extra touch, you can put a small scoop of ice cream on the ice cubes before you pour over the coffee. Stir in the milk, sugar and liqueur, if using. Serve immediately or chill until required.

credits and useful addresses

Angelucci
23b Frith St
London W1V 5TS
Tel 020 7437 5889

Algerian Coffee Stores
52 Old Compton St
London W1V 6PB
Tel 020 7437 2480
www.algcoffee.co.uk
Open since 1887, specialist
suppliers of tea and coffee.
Wide range of coffee-making
equipment.

Aroma Tea and Coffee
Merchants
8a St Marys Place
Shrewsbury SY1 1DZ
Tel 01743 367598
51 Southwater Arcade
Telford TF3 5DZ
Tel 01952 291693

Better Beverage Company
204 Morrison St
Edinburgh EH3 8EA
Tel 0131 476 2600
www.betterbeverage.co.uk

The Bramah Tea and Coffee
Museum
40 Southwark St
London SE1 1UN
Tel 020 7403 5650
www.bramahmuseum.co.uk

Camden Coffee Stores
11 Delancey St
London NW1 7NL
Tel 020 7387 408

The Drury Tea and Coffee
Company
3 New Row
London WC2N 4LH
Tel 020 7836 1960
www.drury.uk.com

Farrers
13 Strickland Gate
Kendal LA9 4LY
Tel 01539 731707
www.farrers.com

Gillards
55 Guild Hall Market
Bath BA2 4AW
Tel 01225 463430

H. R. Higgins (Coffee-Man) Ltd
79 Duke St
London W1K 5AS
Tel 020 7629 3913
Fax 020 7499 5912
enquiries@hrhiggins.co.uk
www.hrhiggins.co.uk

Imperial Teas and Coffees
26 Steep Hill
Lincoln LN2 1LU
Tel 01522 560008

Layton Fern & Co. Ltd
27 Rathbone Place
London W1P 2EP
Tel 020 7636 2237
Fax 020 7580 2869
sales@laytonfern.fsnet.co.uk
www.coffeeisferns.co.uk

Love Saves the Day
Unit G, 18 Smithfield Bldgs
44 Tibb St
Manchester M4 1LA
Tel 0161 832 0777
www.lovesavestheday.co.uk

Markus Coffee Company
13 Connaught St
London W2 2AY
Tel 020 7723 4020

W. Martyn
135 Muswell Hill Broadway
London N10 3RS
Tel 020 8883 5642

The Mecca Tea and Coffee
Merchants
25 Chalybeate St
Aberystwyth SY23 1HX
Tel 01970 612888

Monmouth Coffee Company
27 Monmouth St
London WC2H 9DD
Tel 020 7379 3516
2 Park Street

London SE1 9AB
Tel 020 7645 3585
coffee@monmouthcoffee.co.uk
Coffee roasters and retailers.

The Tea and Coffee Plant
170 Portobello Rd
London W11 2EB
Tel 020 7221 8137

Wilkinsons Tea and Coffee
Merchants
5 Lobster Lane
Norwich NR2 1DQ
Tel 01603 625 121

**THANKS TO THE
FOLLOWING COMPANIES
FOR THE LOAN OF PROPS
FOR PHOTOGRAPHY**

Muji
6–17 Tottenham Court Rd
London W1P 9DP
Tel 020 7323 2208
www.muji.co.jp
Practical and stylish household
items from Japan.

David Mellor
4 Sloane Square
London SW1W 8EE
Tel 020 7730 4259
www.davidmellordesign.co.uk
Specialists in award-winning
cutlery and fine kitchenware.

Helena Rohner
c/Almendro 4
Madrid 28005, Spain
Tel 00 34 91365 7906
Handcrafted tableware in
ceramic and wood.

The Conran Shop
Michelin House
81 Fulham Rd
London SW3 6RD
Tel 020 7589 7401
www.conranshop.co.uk
Design-led home and
kitchenware.

After Noah
121 Upper St
London N1 1QP
Tel 020 7359 4281
www.afternoah.com
An eclectic mix of vintage and
contemporary kitchen and
home ware.

Immaculate House
Old Spitalfields Market
57 Brushfield St
London E1 6AA
Tel 020 7375 1844
Indulgent and decadent
products for the home.

Fortnam and Mason
181 Piccadilly
London W1A 1ER
Tel 020 7973 4147
www.fortnumandmason.co.uk
A wide range of specialist tea
and coffee as well as fine china
and home wares.

Bowles and Linares
32 Hereford Rd
London W2 5AJ
Tel 020 7229 9886
www.bowlesandlinares.co.uk
Beautifully designed coffee
filters, jugs, cups and saucers
made from clear and amber
coloured glass.

Nicole Farhi
17 Clifford St
London W1X 6SL
Tel 020 7494 9051
Carefully chosen eclectic
collection of old and new
products for the home.

FAIRTRADE MOVEMENT

Cafédirect and Teadirect
City Cloisters, Suite B2
196 Old Street
London EC1V 9FR
Tel 020 7490 9520
www.cafedirect.co.uk
Cafédirect and Teadirect are
available in all major multiples,

Planet Organic, Fresh & Wild,
Oxfam and Traidcraft.
Cafedirect and Teadirect are
also sold in all branches of
Costa Coffee across the UK.
Cafédirect buys all its tea and
coffee products direct (hence
the brand name) from the
growers. It is the only company
in the UK to guarantee that
100% of its range carries the
Fairtrade mark and is
committed to setting new
standards for commercial
trading in developing countries.

PICTURE CREDITS

Page 6, below right: Washing
coffee cherries, Cocla co-
operative, Peru / ph Richard
Hide © Cafédirect.

index

acknowledgments

I'd like to thank everyone I have talked to about coffee, particularly Tony Higgins of the excellent H. R. Higgins coffee and tea shop near Oxford Circus in London and David and Liz Phillips, the very knowledgeable owners of The Steamer Trading Cookshop in Lewes (01273 487230) and Alfriston (01323 870055), East Sussex. The Monmouth Coffee Company, in Covent Garden and Borough Market, has always inspired me to explore coffees from all around the world, and, along with Higgins', also a very good shop, features in the photographs in the book. Love Saves the Day in Manchester's Northern Quarter is another place worth seeking out. Many thanks to the Fairtrade organization Cafédirect for images. At Ryland Peters & Small, a big thank you to Alison Starling, Sophie Bevan, Luis Peral-Aranda, Gabriella La Grazie; and to Emily Chalmers and Debi Treloar for making the pictures so beautiful yet drinkably real. Thanks, in general, to my aunt Julia Ellis for bringing me packets and tales from her travels and to Gail and Frances for book hunting.

PUBLISHER'S ACKNOWLEDGMENTS: The publisher would like to thank the Monmouth Coffee Company, H. R. Higgins (Coffee-Man) Ltd and Layton Fern & Co. Ltd for allowing us to photograph in their premises. Thanks also to Cafédirect for the loan of images. cafédirect